HEALING
IN SPIRIT

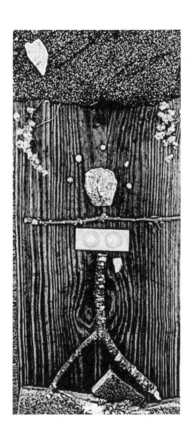

Poems to Comfort and Encourage the Heart

Kathy Stevens Bradley

outskirts
press

Grateful Acknowledgements

So many of my friends and family have inspired me to write these poems and have also encouraged me to gather them into this book, and I greatly appreciate their inspiration and encouragement. I have been given help in so many ways…so I say a special thank you to:

Debbie Daniel and Helen Schell for reading all of my poems, & offering excellent editing suggestions; Heidi, for encouragement and retreat space within which to explore and write, and art therapy on the deck at rehab; "The Wildflowers" for responding with support to my first poems during retreats; my nieces Susy and Jennifer for interest and encouragement; Nancy M. and Mary Gayle for inspired help with struggles; Dr. Chuck, Rafe and all my therapists, doctors, & nurses at HEALTH SOUTH for encouragement and compassion during my stroke; Hilda, for arranging a triage team to meet me at the hospital, and who also ministered at my bedside with Rumi; Colleen, for positive encouragement, running countless errands, packing me up to leave rehab, and driving me home; Harriet, for taking care of my dog Sam, and bringing clothes & other necessities from home; Pam M. for private therapeutic yoga after my stroke; Jack & Debbie for home-cooked meals delivered to rehab, & bedside concerts; Carley for the beautiful birdcage of inspirational thoughts; Cathy for the "magic" stone & bedside encouragement; and to so many who shared conversations or situations that brought forth poems - Cathy, Heidi, Hilda, Jemme, the Burgesses & McCarthys, Mary A., Sandy W, Leigh, Billy, Lockwood, Danny, Fran; Jalal ad Din Muhammed Rumi, and translator Coleman Barks, for inspirational thoughts; Dr. Brene Brown, for her healing book The Gifts of Imperfection; Dr. Jill Bolte, author of My Stroke of Insight, Stacey and Brad, for the peace of City Yoga; Hilda and Jemme for meditative help and sharing at Upstream Mindfulness Practice and Holistic Health & to Ronnie D. for the exquisite photograph of "MARY." And finally, a wow, huge thank you to Colleen Comeau for collecting all this information digitally and helping me with wonderful techno-therapy.

Special thanks to my son Luke, for his love, steady encouragement, and support, as well as my dear daughter-in-law Katie, & grands Annie and Charlie, for love and joy abounding.

And a most special thank you and appreciation to Leonard, for his love and friendship, thoughtful caring and support in all things, large and small.

Table of Contents

Introduction

Years of writing these poems have truly helped me "heal in spirit." It began simply, with a poem I wrote for a school-wide writing activity during my years as an elementary school arts teacher. The poem which resulted was wholly surprising to me! "SPRING", which sounds like a benign topic for creative writing, became my first ever acrostic poem, and brought forth images and feelings that were the opposite of benign. These images got my attention on a deep, personal level.

My interest gained speed not long after, when some personal challenges I was facing had me troubled; a divorce and attempts at reconstructing a satisfying personal life afterwards; my only son leaving for college and the emptiness of the house in his absence; then, the need to sell this "family home," which was much too big for one person now. Some sessions of professional counseling had helped ease my feelings of loneliness; also, the lingering sadness of unsettled "family of origin" wounds and the unsuccessful attempts at finding a partner were eased a bit by these counseling sessions. But as I began writing my acrostic poems, I discovered some excellent therapy that helped quiet and ease my hurting heart, at any time that I was needing comfort, no appointment necessary… in the familiarity of my own living room.

My writing continued to gain momentum, as poems began to be inspired by positive, joyful experiences… and off I would go, scribbling happily, pondering, editing, and re-reading the finished products many times, and using them increasingly as a meditative "jump start." Even though the poems had helped me in stressful times, they were evolving into a satisfying way of recording blessings in my life, and helped me focus on being *thankful*, instead of fearful.

Many of my poems were inspired by friends and discussions we would have, regarding a joy or a dilemma <u>they</u> were going through. I would think about those conversations later, feel moved to write, and then I would share the poem with them, giving them a copy.

There is no denying that acrostic poetry had become an important tool in my emotional expression, as two weeks after I had a serious stroke, I requested a note pad and pen from my nurse at the rehab hospital. I was quietly and desperately trying to grapple with feelings of <u>why</u> this malady would have happened to me, mostly fit and seemingly healthy, at only 60 years old. I cherish the poems written during those first frightening weeks, and the rest of that summer, as they capture my feelings of disbelief and quiet shock. But they *also* expressed the appreciation of <u>having my eyes opened</u> to something previously unnoticed…and that is the world of frightening medical struggles, where patients are dependent upon wheelchairs, walkers, walking canes, prosthetics, intense physical therapy, and life-saving medications. I was *especially thankful*, however, to personally experience the dedication of doctors, nurses, therapists of all types, and hospital helpers. They made such a difference in my outlook about my own medical challenges and enriched my understanding of their devotion to the job, to their *calling* - and I look back with gratitude at the level of compassion and dedication they bring each day, as they show up for "work."

It may seem dramatic to say <u>acrostic poetry has been transformative in my life</u>, but that is the truth. And it is my hope that these poems may support, help, and touch others, touch *you*, as you read them…perhaps "seeing yourself" in some of the feelings expressed, the situations encountered, learning, and hopefully enjoying something you read here.

Maybe you will be inspired to write your own acrostic poem. What is *your* personal passion – running, knitting, tennis, teaching…or volunteering at a food bank? No matter what it is, try writing about it! And on the flip side, as life delivers challenges, that is yet *another* opportunity to write, and possibly gain understanding. Whatever the feelings, there are verbs that could jump onto the page, and thoughts that might surprise you, delight you, or enlighten you. Just sit in your quiet chair with notepad and pen, writing <u>your</u> "thought-provoking" word, vertically on the left side of your page - and see what appears.

Kathy Stevens Bradley
April 2, 2021

What is Acrostic Poetry?

Acrostic poetry is the form featured in my book, and it has become a powerful way to express my feelings, whether I am dealing with challenges or feeling excited about new opportunities. As I was working on publishing this book, I made my first "search" for the word ACROSTIC... and was surprised to find out it was an important writing process that originated with ancient Greek culture! This is how to compose an acrostic:

1. Choose a topic word
2. Write it vertically down the left side of the page
3. Beginning with the first letter, write a sentence that refers to the topic
4. Continue with each letter, staying with the "theme" of thoughts that are emerging

For example:

A writing form I saw my young students enjoying

C ame to be an important part of my own life.

R olling out of my heart, my own thoughts surprise me -

O nto the page they creep, prompted by a single letter.

S o simplistic, yet turning a key to unlock my feelings,

T urning writing time into relaxation or revelation.

I n my quiet chair, with small notebook and pen,

C omes my respite, as I slowly ponder my next word.

During a school-wide writing initiative one year, all teachers and students were asked to write about "spring." I decided to try the technique I had seen on bulletin boards in the 2nd grade hallway, where students had written simple acrostic "name poems." Writing that first poem was when I discovered the *magic* acrostic poetry held for me. Pick a topic word...and try one yourself!

Chapter 1
HEALING IN SPIRIT:

Recognizing, Understanding and
Accepting Childhood Wounds

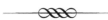

Ancient wounds ache inside me

Nagging at my joys, magnifying my doubts...

X marks the tender spot, quietly throbbing from early fears of not being enough.

I must trust...healing powers also dwell within me.

Every day, I will give myself care and compassion,

Talking to myself gently as I acknowledge mistakes - the way I do with my dear ones.

Yield to the acceptance that I am worthy of being loved... and believe.

Clutching, clinging, courage missing,

Rejecting the notion that I am worthy –

Is it not enough just to be myself?

Tune to my own core and forget the imagined judgment of others.

I have struggled to exhaustion, but my hopeful soul senses:

Comfort is waiting in the arms of my self-acceptance.

Eventually I must admit my jealousy of successes of a friend or colleague-

Negative thoughts coveting others' achievements may reflect my own fears of being inadequate.

Visualizing my traits that need work, I will paint courageous strokes in a confident new light -

Years from now I will be content, quietly proud of the self-portrait I worked to enhance.

Finding my way through frightening experiences or traumatic memories, reminds me I am mortal.

Even in times of triumph, I may be unsettled by my gut's memory of a shock, or hidden weakness.

Accept that I am human and know that this shadow side is part of me,

Reclaiming my courage each time it is challenged … I will continue to honor the wounds within.

No other person can fill me up -

Everything I need is inside me.

Eliminate the constant search for approval and acceptance, remembering...

Disappointment is felt mostly when I try too hard.

Yearn only for self-acceptance; all else will follow.

Remembering yesterday's mistakes can be painful,

Endlessly evaluating what I could have done differently.

Growing past this constant self-blaming, I will strive to fully accept myself-

Renewing my faith, I will focus on today's garden, rather than dwelling on past harvests.

Each day asks me to step out into unknown circumstances -

Trust that wherever I am led, I will plant new seeds… and use the wisdom gained from my past.

Sharing my shadow side scares me to exile … I shut the door.

Hiding who I really am is the strategy, hoping not to drive others away.

Am I to be forever locked alone, in the dark of my deepest heart?

Make room for new life, by boldly opening the window of self-acceptance-

Embracing all parts of myself, I trust that courage and honesty will lead me to light.

MARY, SURFING AWAY ORIGINAL SIN

"Hi Mary,

Hard to believe we've had so many good years together, with you mounted up in my hallway, sending me good vibes every time I walk through the house to my studio or guestroom. And that's a little surprising when I stop and think about it, because as a child, attending a Quaker church in North Carolina, I rarely heard about you, except when we acted out the nativity scene at Christmas time.

So, looking back on that amazing art exhibit thirteen years ago, the one that eventually inspired me to create YOU as an artwork presiding in my home for years, it delights me that I have gotten to know you, Divine Mother. And I came to know you in my own way, which is by using my artist's curiosity and creativity to help me better understand deep personal feelings. Also, there has been the work of reconciling my beliefs and journey toward a fulfilling spirituality, as I have researched the doctrines of traditional theologies. During this search, it has been important for me to guard against randomly throwing out all ideas which are conventional. So, after having this artistic relationship with you, Mary, I realize how important it was to take the time to examine religious symbolism and relate it to my inner life, sifting and finding my personal place in it all. It has been more powerful than I ever imagined. I even rewrote <u>THE LORD'S PRAYER</u> ... as <u>DIVINE MOTHER'S PRAYER,</u> so that it fully resonated with me as a woman, after having experienced wounds from masculine energies in my family of origin. And now, you are on the cover of the first book I have ever published! So Mary, you have deeply inspired me- and you still give me such comfort. I sincerely thank you for that."

The paragraph above closely resembles thoughts I've had from time to time, as I walk by my *"MARY"* artwork (a collage / retablo*) that graces my hallway. During a visit to an art exhibit at the Nasher Museum of Art some years ago, there were many paintings, sculptures, altar pieces…and most of them were religious in subject matter. (Duke University, 2008- EL GRECO TO VELASQUEZ – ART DURING THE REIGN OF PHILIP III) By reading the program notes, I learned for the first time how artists were strictly controlled in expressing their artistic craft in those centuries.

Even though I visit museums frequently, and love learning background facts about paintings, sculptures, artifacts, and lives of the artists, I had never known about the "artistic requirements" placed upon artists in the 15th and 16th centuries by European political rulers and the Catholic Church. As I walked through the exhibit listening to my audio guide, I was somewhat shocked as I heard facts about painters being commanded to depict biblical subjects in precise ways, with exacting requirements. One such formula from authorities was a list of requirements for painting Mary, The Virgin Mother. Four of the non-negotiable rules were 1) she must be walking on water 2) her head must be surrounded with a crown of stars 3) the moon must be shining above her 4) a rosemary bush must be pictured on one side of her body.

Fast forward to an artists' retreat with several friends, one year later. I loved "constructing" things, more so than painting or drawing, and was hoping to make some type of fall collage or mosaic but had no idea exactly what that would be. After breakfast that first day, I left my friends inside the cabin painting and drawing... and slipped out the door into the woodsy mountain yard, hoping for "artistic building materials" to be provided by Mother Nature.

As I walked the gravel driveway, I looked down and immediately saw a rock with a delicate, "picasso-esque" face. Hooray! My collection of art supplies for the day had officially begun. Soon a heart-shaped stone caught my eye. Before long, I pocketed several cherry twigs, a small stick covered with lichen, and some wispy dried flowers that had lingered intact through the fall weather. Then, another heart stone appeared, much smaller than the first.

I was upbeat about the way my "materials search" was proceeding, and as I rounded a corner near the cabin basement, chunks of blue bathroom tile, bumpy orange mosaic tiles, and some roof shingles from an old renovation project seemed to be just waiting for me, along with a big rectangular chunk of lumber, approximately 1' x 3'. I now had an assortment of raw materials that I was excited about, so I headed back into the house to see what could blossom from this collection of new-found treasures. The art retreat was officially in "go mode" for me!

I spread everything out on the porch picnic table, grabbed a sandwich and a bowl of cherries for lunch, and began to eat and ponder. After a while, I had laid the blue tile across the bottom of the board like an ocean, and the cherry tree twigs became a person's body. Topping the body was the beautiful face-rock, and my cherry pits were the stars in her crown. The shingles became the heavens above, and the larger heart stone appeared stage right as the moon. Lo and behold! I realized that I was replicating a version of the "Mary paintings" I had seen at the Nasher Museum! I had not realized the memory of that exhibit was still percolating deep in my mind somehow, as I had walked the mountain property of my friend Heidi.

"MARY, SURFING AWAY ORIGINAL SIN", is the name of the artwork from that long-ago mountain retreat, and that is pictured on the cover of this book. I chose it to be the image for **HEALING IN SPIRIT**, because for me, it relates to the type of tough emotions which brought forth the poems in Chapter 1- anxiety, criticism, fear, envy, regret, and shame. These feelings speak of the fears and insecurities that I experienced, that we _all_ have experienced at some point, and that world religions also point out as troublesome. But, knowing these feelings are *universal* is also to know they are normal, at least in the lesser degrees.

"MARY SURFING AWAY ORIGINAL SIN " also reflects my belief that "original sin" is the psychic burden we receive as we are born to and raised by parents who *themselves* are wounded and struggling, with their own fears and inadequacies… perhaps born into a tumultuous time in history, or in an area in the world experiencing war, famine, racial strife, and other enormous challenges. But I have chosen to picture Mary dealing with these challenges in her own way – by *"surfing"* them - which implies balancing, navigating the waters, standing upright, looking ahead, and handling things … the very best way she can.

As I look back *at MARY, SURFING AWAY ORIGINAL SIN*, and imagine her speaking, she reminds me:

*The cherry pits are my "starry crown", symbolic of the seeds of sweet fruit yet to come, the promise of continued growth, if I continue to seek and try.

* The shingle heavens remind me to be thankful for my home and community, and to recognize even the *smallest* goodness that comes into my life. Sometimes blessings may be as tiny and fragile as those wispy dried flowers in MARY'S sky, but to receive them is still a reason for me to be appreciative.

*The large stone heart, Grandmother Moon, is radiating from the night sky to my heart, which is a receptacle for her beauty and illumination, and continues to remind me of the waxing and waning cycles in the natural world, and my own life.

*The lichen-covered branch, Mary's surfboard, may be enough to keep me afloat in choppy waters, if I absorb the lesson that lichen teaches…that mutually beneficial, cooperative relationships are life-giving, even in some of the harshest environments.

This is Mary's voice, as she has spoken to me…and now maybe she can remind you to surf your own waves and challenges, staying steady, strong, and looking forward.

*RETABLO – Spanish, literally meaning "board behind" - A religious artwork, usually based upon Catholic imagery and symbolism.

Chapter 2
HEALING IN SPIRIT:

Embracing the Love, Care and Wisdom of
Friends and Family

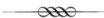

Become acutely aware of my inner needs,

Attending to my physical, emotional, and spiritual selves-

Lest they become weak, quiet, and unable to guide me.

Autumn darkness calls me to rest...

New growth becomes rooted in my intentional stillness and calm.

Curling inward strengthens me, as I gather insights for my next steps -

Emerging later into the light of gained understanding, renewed and wiser in myself.

Clear out attitudes and possessions that don't serve me anymore,

Leaving room in my life for inner growth and simple living.

Energy will flow as I lift the weight from my psyche and my home,

Allowing me to relax within, enjoying lighter heart and mind;

New experiences are welcomed as I clear my cluttered corners.

Coming together to enjoy and weather life's adventures,

Old friends it seems, from the beginning.

Many experiences await, but the predicted course may change-

Positioning the Intuitive Eye will provide the compass,

As this new terrain of togetherness is navigated.

Nothing transforms Two like a shared purpose…

It is a bond girded with hopeful planning and trust.

Oh, the anticipation, joy, and relief - knowing the days will be shared,

No longer searching for an anchor.

Sometimes, though, even the best friend or dear one will not agree -

Here, then, is a toast to gentle honesty that clears the air,

Introducing a new level of intimacy, within which to begin anew.

Powerful devotion and commitment … will continue to grow loving hearts.

Dedicated to Leonard

Communing in the love of friendship and kinship,

Our togetherness creates a snug quilt of support and care...

Never could I be warmed so, naked to life alone.

Now is always the moment to reach for my dear ones-

Eagerly sharing triumphs, or hesitantly confiding shadows, closeness is enriched.

Crises will sometimes enter our circle; by leaning together, we steady ourselves.

Truth-telling in these times of fear or disappointment invites warm trust:

In exchange for exposing our vulnerabilities, the bonds are tightly woven.

Over miles, over years, these resilient strands remain strong,

Nurturing and holding me... gently knitted into my expanding heart.

Come to grips with what must be done –

Over-thinking just wastes precious time.

Undertake the task, one step after another,

Reclaiming my balance with truthfulness.

Action brings energy and direction,

Giving my life a new focus.

Emancipate myself now, by bravely speaking my heart!

Fear creeps in, during times of doubt or struggle-

All confidence in expectations becomes suspect.

Intuition whispers though, reminding me that mysteries are unfolding-

Telling me softly again, the Universe is a bounty of creation.

Hold tight to my belief: miracles are unpredictable, but plentiful.

Freedom is mine, to let go of time-worn pain and hurt –

Old wounds need to heal, even if scars remain:

Rewinding the past endlessly keeps me stuck.

Go forward instead, with joy and anticipation,

Inviting new parts of my life to appear.

Vibrant sunlight will brighten old shadows, and illuminate the path I walk –

Emerging from dark woods to an open sky and heart.

Going quietly inside myself to listen,

Intuitively I know…there is a need, a time, to help and be helped.

Visiting others in my heart is the first step…and I realize

In a reversal of fate, I too, can be in a needy, sorrowful place.

Now is the time for action: share my service, my talents, my gifts,

Girding others in hope – by living the kindness of warm, loving community.

(Written for the United Way fundraising campaign of 2012)

Grab the people, pursuits, and opportunities that ignite my passions –

Reaching for the stars is a life-long endeavor, regardless of age.

Ossifying habits can be put aside lovingly,

Widening me inside for unknown joys to come.

Intuition will guide my next steps to fulfilling endeavors:

Not knowing the way is the way I will arrive,

Growling "go for it!" … my new cry as a life-seeking warrior.

Oh, how I realize this lifetime is limited, but the berry is still sweet.

Up until the last moment of starlight, I will bravely live these words,

Taking pleasure in the wonders that light me from within.

Honor what I know is true in my heart!

Out of my insides and into the world, I will speak it kindly:

Nothing must compromise my courage to express what is within.

Earlier times have witnessed me hiding what I felt, from fear or guilt-

Submerging those emotions deadened me, leaving me unknown to others.

Truths revealed today will fuel my strength to continue stepping forward:

Yesterday's reluctance has yielded the training ground … for a braver self today.

Jump into new experiences that call to me,

On fire by the excitement of learning and expanding myself.

Yes! Staying alive to my passions and curiosity is the portal to vitality.

Putting my hand in yours, a wish for someday soon,

Attests to my faith that I will love again.

Reveling in touch, breath, laughter and sharing,

Together-activities will soon become customs.

Not to worry - perfection will not know either of us…

Each day will offer chances to begin again, by understanding more.

Reveal your face to me, as the sun bursts forth from shadows.

Playing tirelessly without noticing the time passing,

Avalanches of ideas cascade and multiply.

See the delight, attention, and effort that is freely given,

So that a garden, painting, poem, recipe, or song comes into being.

I delve wholeheartedly into the energy and wonder of my discoveries,

Only pausing to smile, romp, and dance with my newest fascination.

Now is the moment I relish, as I commit to the creation that is firing my soul!

Putting aside my need to control, I acknowledge the Universe is in charge.

Accepting the pace of my life brings freedom, as I am learning

Time is a gift to be appreciated … never just relentlessly measured.

Invite the natural unfolding of things, not judging by clock or calendar-

Every day, this way, can be a revelation and its own gift.

Now is the Eternity I crave and am realizing is held in each minute:

Come to this awareness with arms open and face upward,

Embracing what is given to me!

Plow my energy into my calling-

Underestimating it would diminish my chance to share

Revel in the opportunity to offer my gifts,

Placing value on all I have been taught.

Offering my thoughts and experiences to others makes me hopeful –

Shining my light may illuminate the darkness for someone, somewhere.

Encouraging this harvest is my chosen path now.

Oh! For guidance to come –

Pulling me out of my fear,

Enveloping me with the love and courage

Needed to find my way.

My joy in who I am, is the key…

Even accepting the parts I want to hide.

Remember that my old life was not containing me,

Even though it gave me such purpose for a time.

Beginning again with slow steps and courage,

Insights will come for new ways of being in the world

Revealed to me by loved ones, sages, rain, rocks, and mulled memories,

Telling me to trust ... all is as it should be.

Heroic journeys may begin with trembling feet; and at sunrise, I will continue on.

R eaching down, deep inside myself,

E nergy is ready and waiting:

I t is time for a creative life movement.

N ever mind that some questions are unanswered-

V irtually every cell is alive with anticipation,

E xcitedly awaiting each new day's adventure.

N ow is my opportunity for courageous trail-blazing,

T raveling with gratitude along my own soul's satisfying path.

Re-imagining my life, I will allow my interests to follow a new path –

Every beginning has its end, even though changes may feel strange at first.

Time has come to appreciate- but let go of - what has been,

Inviting a new and meaningful structure to come forth.

Remember: just as new seeds planted need time to sprout and take root,

Eventually I will relax into a new stage of life, my chance to grow again.

T aking thoughtful care to assist life is holy work.

E very living plant or creature thrives when aided-

N o child, flock, garden, or friendship flourishes without help.

D evotion, day in and day out, tills the fertile ground.

I n go the seeds of gentle effort - watching and watering, the blooms appear.

N o grand gestures or rescues are necessary:

G iving attention - mindfully, regularly, unobtrusively – enables healthful growth.

Place my hands over my heart to quiet myself,

Releasing pressures that I must find answers alone.

Ask for faith, guidance, understanding-

Yet be patient if these do not appear quickly.

Each visit with the Divine can nourish and calm me,

Remembering: I am never lost when I return to my Spirit home.

(I wrote the following "Divine Mother's Prayer" as a personal substitute for "The Lord's Prayer," in 2008.)

Divine Mother's Prayer

Our Mother, who is all around us,

Comforting is your name.

Your blessings come, your miracles done,

On Earth, as throughout Creation.

Give us this day the bread and wine,

And remind us to help others,

As we recall those who have helped us

And tended us gently.

And lift us up to Inspiration,

Opening our hearts and our minds -

For you are the warmth, and the wisdom,

And the nourishment for our blossoming souls,

Forever and always, Amen.

Kathy Stevens Bradley 2008

Chapter 3
HEALING IN SPIRIT:

Experiencing Support, Blessings, and Hope during Medical Trauma

———⬡⬡⬡———

My Stroke Journey

"Saturday morning had begun joyfully, playing fiddle music with friends at an outdoor market; next sunset I was in a hospital bed, having suffered a stroke at age 60. My first day in rehab, I waited in a wheelchair for therapy, hoping to regain use of my speech, left hand, arm, and leg… feeling pitiful. I heard a boy's voice and looked up; a teenager nearby was learning to operate two new prosthetic arms. My situation was put into perspective – I quickly prayed 'thank you' for my blessings, then prayed for the young man with new limbs."

The previous paragraph was written on May 4ᵗʰ, 2014 - exactly one year after my stroke. <u>Reader's Digest</u> had sponsored a "100 - word writing challenge," and I accepted that challenge by writing about the most dramatic emergency of my life, a serious stroke which paralyzed the left side of my body. I thought perhaps the essay would educate more people about the damage of strokes, and how to better prevent them.

Few TV shows or movies portray strokes, so unfortunately most people have no understanding of the damaging effects that can result, including partial paralysis of the face, hands, arms, legs; also, diminished speech and /or eyesight abilities, along with possible impaired recall of common words, symbols, and facts. When a blood clot moves to the brain and lodges in a blood vessel, blood flow is cut off from areas "downstream" that supply specific nerves and muscles, causing them to cease functioning.

In my case, I immediately suspected I was having a stroke, and a music friend quickly drove me to the closest ER. I was examined by a doctor during the first 15 minutes, and the doctor ordered a CAT scan which showed nothing. An hour later, she refused to administer an MRI (which I <u>now</u> know is the conclusive test to determine a stroke). She said firmly, "I don't think we really need that… plus, it's a $7,000 test!" Of course, filled with panic and already experiencing some weird "kaleidoscope" vision, limping on my left leg, and speaking with slurred speech, <u>I was not coherent nor forceful enough in that situation to be my own advocate.</u>

Even though I was still speaking with slurred speech, and limping on my left leg, the doctor released me (4 hours later) with a diagnosis of *"fluid in the inner ear"*. I had been sent home without the benefits of the "clot-busting" medication that could have been administered to me, (thrombolytics) and which would have prevented serious stroke damage. Waking up at home the next morning, my entire left side was cold to the touch, and my left hand, arm, and leg were paralyzed. I called my doctor friend Hilda, and was taken to a different hospital this time, and accurately diagnosed with an ischemic (clot) stroke…but it was <u>too late</u> for the medications I could have received the day before; my paralysis was a reality.

On my 3ʳᵈ day in the hospital, a cheerful, energetic woman came bouncing into my room, saying "Hello, my name is Joy, and I work for a rehab hospital next door. You can begin your recovery with us! We have excellent physical, occupational, and speech therapists…and you will be supervised by doctors, nurses, and counselors who are especially skilled with stroke patients. You would begin as a "resident" patient for 2 weeks, living at the rehab hospital, and then you would move back home. You would then <u>continue your rehabilitation</u> at our facility 3 days a week, with carefully planned out-patient care." It took me all of 2 seconds to say (with slurred speech) "Sign me up!" It sounded like the perfect next step for me, as I knew nothing about rehab, and was totally in the dark about maximizing my recovery.

For two weeks as an inpatient, and three months as an outpatient, the doctors, nurses, therapists, and counselors at HEALH SOUTH REHABILITATION HOSPITAL (Columbia, SC) ministered to me with kindness, compassion, patience, and humor…all of which I needed in great amounts. I entered rehab quietly terrified that I might never walk or dance again or be able to play guitar with my friends…but thanks to those medical professionals, I finally learned to move my arm and grasp a tennis ball, and after two months, I was able to walk a complete lap around the rehab gym, very slowly and proudly, without the use of a walker or cane. My group of doctors and nurses, physical therapists and counselors had embraced me as a whole person, attending to both my *physical <u>and</u> emotional needs*…and it made all the difference.

Also, other stroke survivors, my "fellow travelers" with whom I shared time in our stroke activity groups, helped me realize…there is <u>always</u> an opportunity for hope, laughter, and making new friends, regardless of the circumstances. Today, March 3rd, 2021 at this writing, I am only 2 months away from marking the 8th anniversary of my stroke and celebrating my incredible recovery. I have fully recovered my guitar playing capabilities, and yes, I can now dance! I wholeheartedly thank <u>all</u> the energetic, caring souls at HEALTHSOUTH, who rescued my spirit and rehabilitated my body, during the most challenging time of my life.

For more information: *American Heart Association; heart.org*

Ischemic stroke = clot   **Hemorrhagic stroke** = brain bleeding (*Treatments & medications vary between the two)*

Signals from a quiet part of my body awakened me-

Transforming me fearfully at first, then profoundly in spirit...

Rearranging my priorities into a rightful order.

Over time, my moments had become frenetically packed,

Keeping me preoccupied, blocked - from Mother Earth's simple blessings.

Each sunrise now reminds me...dip deeply, gently, slowly and savor life's simple delights.

Hope is administered in large doses as you tend me:

Each day, your eyes and hands encourage,

Always ready with a new idea, technique, exercise for strengthening.

Love for me, for humanity, is shown in the gentleness of your caring-

Every laugh and tear shared together is part of your wellness elixir;

Recovery, and my new life, are possible as you answer your calling.

All in... is the mantra of the true competitor.

Total immersion in salty sweat, tears, fight, and fatigue

Helps to galvanize the strength required.

Lap after lap, layers of belief begin building-

Eventually, a new shape, life, destiny takes form.

The commitment in pursuing the goal is what betters me -

Each day, aided by my stamina, is training time for victory.

Soothing my soul, as well as caring for my body's needs,

I deeply crave the drink that only you can bring.

Stepping in gently with your listening eyes, laughter, poetry, and prayers,

Together we transcend the fears as you tend me.

Each beautiful face blends with caring arms that hold and comfort me-

Rivers of grace have flowed into my life by knowing your love.

So blessed am I, realizing our paths will continue to meet in the labyrinth's center.

Reinventing my old life into the new is a miracle I can participate in -

Examining unhealthy attitudes, I focus on long-held, hardwired habits.

Sadness at losing familiar ways wells up though,

Until I stop and admit, those ways often worked against me.

Realization: this chance to reassess is a rare event and should be welcomed!

Rough times hone me, like sandpaper on the oak board.

Every challenge offers the work, but also the reward-

Courage is needed to make these changes, however.

Telling myself this is an opportunity, not a demotion,

I am ready to see with new eyes and live new possibilities.

Of all the directions my life would take, I never predicted this one...

Now, I rise earnestly to meet the occasion.

(I recorded lots of feelings and conversations in a notebook at the HealthSouth Rehabilitation Center, and these are recollections of a conversation I had with "Dr. Chuck" on May 17, 2013, which inspired my poem RESURRECTION.)

Dr. Chuck came in and asked me how the music was last night, (my "music-picking" friends had come and played for me in the garden) and I said GREAT! He said, "It seems like there are a lot of people who love you." I responded that one of the "up" sides of this situation (stroke) is that it's like being able to attend your own funeral… people are so helpful, going to great lengths to show you they care, bringing you food, flowers, cards, just generally letting you how much you are loved and appreciated.

He said, "Let's not think of it as a funeral, because you're still alive…how about a 'resurrection?' Because <u>you're</u> <u>not</u> <u>dead</u>, but that old idea that you are 'bullet proof'…that idea has died. You can no longer view yourself that way. But that's OK, because… it never was true! And it is interesting, isn't it, that we mourn a lie? Try to accept that the bullet proof idea <u>never</u> <u>was</u> <u>true</u>, and now you've been 'resurrected' …and you can see the truth of that. So, you can adjust your life to that reality, and live accordingly."

Bless you, Dr. Chuck. You are a true doctor of Wholeness.

Slowly relax and deep breathe,

Understanding that no command performance is waiting -

Realizing that my life can unfold,

Revealing itself in each successive moment.

Every act and react is a creature's life,

Not needing the measuring and judging of others.

Dear sweet Universe and those who love me…my deepest thanks!

Each new day, and every breath of support

Reassures me to let go, rest, and enjoy.

Hallelujah for the energy I feel pulsing through my body -

Eat, sleep, move, rest, cry and laugh like my life depends on it!

All the earthly pleasures that are most satisfying seem to be simple -

Remind myself to retreat quietly and regularly to count these blessings.

Today is my birthday - each day - if I remember to live in gratitude.

A Letter of Profound Thanks

(Sent to my family, friends, students, doctors, nurses, and therapists, May 14, 2014)

I have marked the year anniversary of my stroke and feel very blessed to have come through it all so well. There is no way to adequately describe how it felt to me, to receive so many healing & encouraging acts of kindness from you all. I am certain that <u>each</u> of you played an important role in my recovery; to know that I was not alone in my journey to become functional and "well" again was crucial, keeping me upbeat, positive, and motivated to work toward recovery.

<u>Some of my beautiful memories:</u>

(Recalled from my time at Richland Palmetto Hospital and HealthSouth Rehabilitation Hospital, Columbia, S.C.)

- family and friends holding my hands, praying for me, on the first days of my stroke
- home-cooked meals brought into my room at the rehab hospital
- ukulele concerts on my hospital bed; fiddle & banjo concerts in the garden
- a unique, hand-crafted walking cane delivered in person for Mother's Day
- new art supplies and art therapy, outdoors on the rehab deck
- meditation lessons in the prayer room
- a full cosmetic bag with new goodies delivered on Day 1 of rehab, so I could beautify
- new yoga clothes to wear for rehab
- new decorative pillow and "cuddle blankie" for my hospital bed
- letters and drawings from my students, delivered by a teacher friend
- two students and their mom chanting a meditation song for me on rehab deck
- a <u>miracle plan</u> quickly put into action, as I couldn't travel to my son's law school graduation ceremony… an angel friend arranged for a meeting room (at the rehab hospital), a potluck meal, and big screen viewing, inviting 12 family friends to gather, eat, and digitally watch my sweet son walk across the stage to receive his law degree.

And that wasn't all!

The first day back home, after my two residential weeks at HealthSouth Rehab:

- my house had been cleaned for me
- belongings were carried to a downstairs bedroom, as I could not navigate stairs yet
- a friend/food website was created, & delicious homemade meals arrived at dinner time
- cheerful flowers, cards, letters, phone calls, visits
- help sorting out & organizing hospital invoices
- books and personal stories about positive stroke recoveries were provided
- <u>3 months of car rides</u> to and from the rehab hospital & dr. appointments were scheduled and provided (as I was unable to drive for 4 months)
- <u>Private restorative yoga lessons</u> were provided by my yoga teacher-friend

<u>What an amazing list of deeds!</u>

You all taught me, there are so many ways to respond and give help…each of which is valuable to a person in need. I appreciate all your many kindnesses, and I intend to respond whenever needed, and "pay it forward" every single chance I get.

I appreciate you sticking with this long letter, but it is only long because my heart is overflowing. I wanted to celebrate and appreciate- IN WORDS- the beauty of my family, old friends, new friends, medical helpers, colleagues, and students.

Bless you…and thank you.
Kathy Stevens Bradley

Grace has been a kindly visitor in different seasons of my life,

Reaching out to hand me gifts - some beautifully shiny, exhilarating, joyful -

At other times leaving dark presents - odd, unexpected, or fearful - hidden in many layers.

Taking up my courage to unwrap those completely is my exercise in faith.

I am asked to use my stillness, my patience, my quiet tenacity.

Threading in and around all of these, is the illuminating power of sweet, gentle time.

Unwavering belief in the power of this mystery is calming and lightens my days.

Divine assistance continues to arrive at my door with a whisper, a soft tap, or a loud knock -

Entreating me to trust, open the portal, and let blessings step in.

Chapter 4
HEALING IN SPIRIT:

Experiencing Nature's Beauty and Learning from her Wisdom

Coveted above its three-leaved brethren is the prized four-leaf,

Locked in its mound - waiting for a calm, hopeful eye.

Of all symbols, this one boldly promises luck.

Value the patience to stop, kneel, hunt,

Especially when each day's minute has its perceived task.

Relaxing enough to pause and slowly examine is, inherently … the blessed reward.

Can I remember what my Mother Earth teaches me,

Over and under every step I take?

Now is the time to look, smell, touch, listen, and breathe!

Notice the tiny, intricate, rough, and shiny-

Exalt the enormous, ancient, and mysterious.

Coming back daily to her sensory gifts,

Take in her lessons of variety, strength, flexibility, and co-existence.

Embrace all creatures and creations of this world…

Divinity is here!

Floating in and filling up my house, the waters have changed my life–

Lost, the security of my serene retreat, the orderly and familiar surroundings.

Outside in the trash now lay precious photos, mementos, and personal treasures, wet and broken.

On the surface, devastation; but dive beneath and see kindnesses flowing like a river, neighbor to neighbor, to friends, to strangers–

Divine healing grace has baptized me…with a new vision of cherished and caring community.

Dedicated to Jim, Katie, and Bryann Burgess, and all the courageous citizens of Columbia, SC

October 3–6, 2015

Mother Nature gave me a job I take seriously -

Always my eyes are watchful, my intuition active:

My role is to protect and guide my cub.

All potential threats will draw my tooth, my claw.

Be advised: I know this charge is for now, and not forever-

Each babe will grow to adulthood and fight its own battles.

At creature-core, however, will be self-worth and dignity,

Reinforced in early years by a loving parent on duty.

Making time for mindful non-doing quiets my stress.

Each day offers me a chance to practice again, by noticing my world at a tranquil pace –

Dipping deeply into measured breath, warm teacup steam, bee-hum of sunlit cherry blossoms,

I become still … as I slow myself … allowing full baptism into my surroundings.

Teaching myself that I need this pause each day is a challenge, though-

As I have absorbed well, my culture's lesson to be a "multi-tasking marvel."

Today however, and each day forward, I have the chance of a lifetime:

Experiencing my life in all its richness, as I learn to live it moment - by - moment.

Marveling in the ways of the Universe,

Yet unable to comprehend, I pray -

Stay in faith, stay in faith, stay in faith.

Things unseen and unmeasured are strongly felt,

Evidence that the invisible is tangible.

Rich in wisdom, nature reveals abundant miracles -

Yea, though I do not understand, I believe.

Purple spikes sway, as the butterfly bush dances -

Each sense seems to awaken, once I stop, attend, absorb.

A tea-olive breeze perfumes my arm as I write,

Cloud guardians float by slowly, without watching or intruding.

Euphoria's price is so reasonable… just – slow – myself … and BE.

Seeing the waters with new eyes,

Ancient worlds connect with my life today.

Putting me in touch with my place on this Earth.

Every day and Eternity are reconciled somehow,

Lifted by those who love, learn, and share the life of this place -

Open doors to sacred spaces, and mesmerizing creatures, have appeared to me.

Sapelo Island is a barrier island off the southern coast of Georgia and is accessible only by aircraft or boat. It is the site of the last known Gullah community, Hogs Hammock. Also located there is The University of Georgia Marine Institute, which focuses on research and education. I was blessed to spend a week there in 2011, as part of teacher recertification course.

Such love for you two cannot be held in this small sky.

How generously the heavens share happy tears for your day,

Offering a downpour, filling the wedding cups with nature's fine drink.

Watery wishes flow for your days to be gentle together,

Even though clouds will allow enough sun for strong, steady growth.

Remember… refresh each other in times of drought, as they are inevitable, as are

Storms, which will dissipate as you clasp hands, walking through them together.

Stone aged people anticipated, anxiously preparing for changes –

Predicted the vernal equinox with quiet, careful sky-watching.

Rejoicing with rituals, they welcomed the return of light and warmth.

Ingeniously they set stones, created calendars and celebration circles.

New centuries later, our needs no different, we sense the sun shifting-

Green season, we sing your arrival with joy and relief!

(My first acrostic poem , written at Brennen Elementary School)

Yearning for my life to be strong and positive,

One path has appeared, leading to flexible body and mind, and tranquility within.

Gaining insight from my teachers, I slowly absorb wisdom the Ancients knew...

All human spirit is felt within my cells, muscles, nerves, blood, and bones.

Author's Bio

Kathy Stevens Bradley has enjoyed writing acrostic poetry for almost 20 years. This type of expressive writing was especially helpful when she had an unexpected stroke at age 60. Her 38 years as an elementary school arts teacher (music, drama, & visual arts) in Columbia, S.C. were busy and joyful year. She had the opportunity to write and produce numerous plays and video productions for and sometimes *with* her elementary school students. She also wrote and co-produced the 6-part social studies series, <u>Detective Bonz & The S.C. History Mystery</u>, which is presently viewed on SCETV's educational website *knowitall.org*. Some of her favorite pastimes are playing guitar, writing, painting, walking, and spending time with her grandchildren, family, and pups. She is hoping that her two grands will soon be her cohorts in singing and making up new songs. Kathy is presently employed as a writer with SCETV.